How To Do SEO For Beginners and Pros In The New AI-Driven World

Roggie Clark

Get Your SEO Agency Together With This Book

The truth is, a lot of people get into SEO because they think it's an easy job, but don't have the slightest clue about the business and how it actually works. So their agency or consultant career is D.O.A. before it even starts — this book can prevent that by getting you started off right, especially in this new AI world we live in.

https://www.amazon.com/dp/B0FFJVS5H7

Learn More SEO From Me

Below, I included links to several SEO books I've written. They are excellent reads.

The ABCs of SEO: Search Engine Optimization 101

https://www.amazon.com/ABCs-Search-Engine-Optimization-Page-ebook/dp/B0C2JSLW7M

The Technical SEO Handbook

https://www.amazon.com/Technical-SEO-Handbook-Learn-Issues-ebook/dp/B0CMBJR9QV

The SEO and Web Developer Collaboration Guide

https://www.amazon.com/SEO-Web-Developer-Collaboration-Guide-ebook/dp/B0DHLBM48C

Learn HTML and Javascript From Me

The Basics of JavaScript Coding For Beginners: Learn Basic JavaScript Programming Concepts in less than 50 pages

https://www.amazon.com/Basics-JavaScript-Coding-Beginners-Programming-ebook

The Basics of HTML (Hypertext Markup Language) Coding For Beginners: Learn Foundational HTML Programming Concepts

https://www.amazon.com/Basics-Hypertext-Markup-Language-Beginners-ebook

Learn HTML, CSS, and JavaScript With This One Book

To learn all three coding languages, check out the full book.

https://www.amazon.com/Basics-Front-End-Development-HTML-JavaScript-ebook/dp/B0DJ147B15

Consulting, Coaching Services, Or Podcast Appearances

I know that from reading this book, it simply may not be enough information for you; you may require more personalized support with your unique business situation, or you want to share my thoughts along with your content. So, because of that, I'm offering the opportunity to receive consulting, coaching, and podcast appearances from me on SEO and AI. As far as coaching and consulting, I can offer support with:

- Creating SOPs (Standard Operating Procedures)
- Creating SEO strategies
- Content Suggestions
- Technical Audits
- Web design/migrations
- Competitor analysis
- Keyword research
- SEO Career Coaching

For podcasting, I can:

- Set up a paid podcast appearance or guest blog post with me, with a contract in writing, with dates, times, and resources that are needed from you.
- Help with the promotion of said podcast after I finish appearing in it.

- Provide discounted copies of any of my SEO or Web Developer books and negotiate a royalty payment split in exchange for acting as an affiliate for my books, courses, templates, etc.

If you are interested in any of these services or collaboration opportunities, and would like to request more information for a specific need you may have.

Please email me at **bouncerankseo@gmail.com**. In your email, please include the following information:

- Your name
- The business you represent (if applicable)
- Team size (if applicable)
- What service or collaboration opportunity do you want
- Any other important information I should know about you

My administrative assistant will email you back within 24 - 48 hours with rates and an information sheet for you to review. Thank you so much for your time and interest in working with me!

College or University Usage

SEO is still a booming industry with no chance of slowing down, even with AI in the mix (kudos to the higher learning institutions for offering courses to teach this subject), and this book is my way of helping to make it easier.

I recommend that college deans and professors consider this book for their curriculum and as a resource for their students to use for their research. If you want to use the text for your course or have your bookstore source it for students to purchase, you can contact me directly.

Please email me at **bouncerankseo@gmail.com**. In your email, please include the following information:

- Your name
- The school you represent
- The class size you are teaching
- The length of your course (e.g. 6-week course, 12-week course, etc.)
- Any other important information I should know

My administrative assistant will email you back within 24 - 48 hours with rates and an information sheet to use for your class.

Copyright

Title: How To Do SEO For Beginners and Pros In The New AI-Driven World
Author: Roggie Clark

Cover Design: Roggie Clark
Editing: Renee' Clark

Printed in the United States of America

Disclaimer

The views and opinions expressed in this book are those of the author and do not necessarily reflect the official policy or position of any individual, company, or organization cited or referenced in the text.

The author is not affiliated with any of the individuals, companies, or organizations mentioned in the text, nor does the author receive any form of compensation for citing or referencing them. Some sample scenarios in this text are fictitious. Any similarity to actual persons, living or dead, is coincidental.

The professional information (strategies, tips, and concepts) in this text is distributed on an "as is" basis, without warranty. While every precaution has been taken in the preparation of the text to ensure all information is accurate, neither the author nor the publisher shall have any liability to any person or entity with respect to any loss or damage caused or alleged to be caused directly or indirectly by the instructions contained in this text or by the computer software and hardware products described in it.

Neither the author nor the publisher guarantees any specific results or outcomes, and the information provided in this text should not be construed as professional advice. Readers should always consult with a qualified professional before making any significant changes to their website or business.

By reading this text, you agree that the author nor the publisher is responsible for any direct, indirect, incidental, or consequential damages that may arise from the use of the information provided. You assume full responsibility for any actions taken based on the information presented in this text.

Table of Contents

Introduction

If you're reading this book, you're probably already feeling the ground shift beneath your feet. AI is everywhere: in restaurants, on TV screens, in cars. Just like that, it has become part of everyday life. AI is all the rage, and search engines have gone all in.

Now, chatbots are being used to answer queries directly on search engines, and yet, marketers are promising the same results using the latest tools and tactics that are specifically targeted to achieve success in this new "AI era". But here's the thing: none of that changes the fundamentals. Organic marketing still matters, and so does the role of a skilled SEO professional.

The mistake many make is assuming that AI can replace organic marketing/SEO or that the latest AI tactic will automatically deliver results. It cannot. AI is a tool, not a substitute for relationships, authority, or quality content.

SEO is not dead. It is changing. And the role of an SEO professional is changing with it. I want to let you know from the beginning: this is not going to be what you normally expect from a book about AI and SEO.

Most books, videos, and blogs I've seen cover the same predictable topics, and go on and on about all the new jargon and lingo: AEO this, GEO this, ChatGPT prompts that, how to get cited by an AI bot, or how adding a

"TLDR" might somehow help content get chosen by AI. This stuff has its place, and I'm not saying they aren't useful. But this book is about something different.

The problem is, when people hear "SEO," they often treat it as interchangeable with "organic marketing." In many ways, that makes sense. But by focusing too narrowly on SEO tactics alone and now AI-driven SEO tactics, the larger conversation around organic marketing has been hijacked. We're now flooded with discussions that have little to do with whether a business actually succeeds in this so-called "AI-driven world."

Now, all the talk is about showing up for some irrelevant AI overview; that conversation about how to actually get a real person to someone's website just went completely out the window. AI is not even half the puzzle. You can optimize all you want for AEO and GEO, but if a customer comes to a website and it lacks substance, meaning, and life in general, no doubt they are going to leave, and you are well on your way to losing clients.

So what I am saying is it's time to cut the "chit-chat" (pun intended) and instead get back to the basics, and that is what it really takes to organically market a business, and since SEO intersects so much with this, it's a must we begin to refocus the conversation back to talking about how to do organic marketing with SEO and AI as the backdrop and no longer as the forefront.

In other words, it's time to take it back to the early days of the internet, when real people did the talking and meaningful insights that can be actively applied were shared.

So, this book is about what marketing a business looks like today—how to truly market organically while navigating this new AI landscape. I'm not saying AI is useless. It has its place, and it can be incredibly helpful. But SEO and AI should work together, not compete for attention.

My concern is that there is an obsession with the latest AI trick or hack, as if that alone guarantees success. This leads to businesses getting so caught up in these tactics that they lose sight of the bigger picture.

The result? Many businesses still fail, even after fully embracing AI. Why? Because these tactics alone don't create sustainable success. True, long-term success comes from creating meaningful connections with customers, something no AI chatbot can replicate.

So again, let me be clear: this is not a book about AI tactics. There are plenty of books that dive into AI technology, tools, and prompts. And it's not about bashing AI either—like I said, it has its place. This book is about how to get organic traffic in an AI world, without losing sight of what actually makes businesses succeed.

I felt called to write a book like this because I know people still love SEO. They love helping businesses get found naturally. They enjoy the challenge and the joy of making something visible to the right audience. That hasn't changed. What has changed is the environment.

As SEOs, we cannot forget our purpose: to get clients meaningful, sustainable, organic traffic. That is what the best SEOs do.

AI may shift the landscape, and we'll need to adapt to it, but our mission stays the same. Businesses will always need ways to reach people. Commerce isn't going away. Business models will evolve, strategies will change, and AI will play a role, but the fundamentals of connecting people with products and services will always matter.

So this book is for those of us who want to do things differently. If you're looking for the latest AI tricks or "growth hacks," this is not that book. This is for those who want to go deeper: how to get clients' traffic, deliver real results, and remain valuable as a professional even in this new AI-driven era.

I can't control which clients stay or leave, and neither can you. But we can control how we adapt. For me I learned from working with top-level enterprises and corporations. Eventually, I had to step out and build my own path. That experience shaped this book.

Okay, with that said, let's start with Chapter 1. I want to dive into more detail about this new AI landscape, how we got here, and just what my overall thoughts are.

I am sharing this here to help you pull back the layers and declutter your mind from all the rhetoric going on about AI and SEO. This will help prime your mind so you can get back to focusing on clients and not obsessing over trying to master all these AI tactics.

Chapter 1: Rethinking Organic Marketing in the AI Era

For years, SEO professionals have been trained to chase rankings. Optimize the page. Get the link. Hit the keyword. Write the blog post. Speed up the website. But in the last couple of years, something has changed; now all the SEO tactics are focused on AI.

You see, in the past, agencies and consultants could get big results with just a handful of blog posts and a few basic landing pages. That was enough to see meaningful SEO wins. But over time, the game changed. More content was required to get the same impact, and then once AI got involved, everything shifted again. Suddenly, it wasn't about reaching people anymore; it was about "generative optimization" and gaming chatbot-style tools.

The tactics became increasingly complex and, frankly, ridiculous. Blog posts ballooned in size, filled with recycled "question keywords" scraped from search results, just to tick boxes for algorithms. Agencies invested in endless tools, spammed forums, and eventually leaned on AI tools or cheap outsourced writers instead of real experts. On paper, it looked like a shortcut, but in practice, content got worse, traffic declined, and engagement fell flat.

Users themselves started tuning out. Top results no longer guaranteed trust or conversions, and people grew skeptical of auto-generated summaries and AI-fed answers.

The promise of "perfect traffic" at the top of search results disappeared. The truth is, people don't trust search results like they once did, and AI hasn't replaced genuine interest or connection.

This should be a wake-up call for SEO professionals who thought that being "ahead of the curve" meant obsessing over algorithms and chasing the latest tricks. That old image of the hoodie-wearing SEO locked in a dark room with charts and dashboards is done. Success now demands something else: social intelligence, audience understanding, and a focus on people, not just keywords.

SEO isn't about flexing tactics, spitting out reports, or throwing gimmicks at clients. It's about objectives, not vanity metrics. Agencies that obsess over rankings while ignoring user needs are missing the point. Businesses don't always need more traffic; they need to make better use of the traffic they already have. Bloggers don't need to churn out thousands of words; they need posts people actually want to read.

The bigger problem is that search has always been more about profitability than quality. If you need proof, look at recipe searches: bloated, copy-paste posts stuffed with backlinks, ranking high despite offering nothing of real value. Bad content that checks all the "SEO boxes" still underperforms, because users can smell when something lacks originality or insight. Add AI rehashing into the mix, and you just accelerate the problem.

Some argue the answer is to pivot from "informational" to "transactional" keywords, but that still sidesteps the real issue. Content that ignores originality and client needs will always fail, no matter the keyword strategy. Agencies reusing the same AI templates across clients prove this; everything starts to sound the same, and results spiral downward.

The truth is, people don't care about ranking or follower counts anymore. They care about authenticity. They want original voices, not regurgitated copy. Ranking number one doesn't automatically make you a thought leader anymore; it just means you played the system, and people can smell B.S.

Again, this should be a wake-up call. Lazy SEO doesn't work. Obsessive SEO doesn't work. Exploiting other professionals doesn't work. Denial doesn't work. The industry has to rethink its foundation, and not just dump everything on AI. Rankings are meaningless if they don't translate into actual customers.

Yes, SEO tactics, strategies, and methods still have value — even the AI-driven ones. But if all you do is chase algorithms, your work is vulnerable. This is exactly why, when AI came in the door of SEO, everyone started obsessing over it, and started losing sight of what really matters, and that is delivering organic traffic.

Search engines change, AI evolves, and what worked last month may not work this month. As SEO professionals, we are well accustomed to this constant shift, but to just reduce organic marketing, an art as much as it is a science, down to a series of AI prompts? I don't think that's right.

True organic marketing is about building visibility in ways that last. It is about creating content and experiences that your audience finds valuable, earning attention, trust, and engagement naturally.

Again, not just setting up some AI-driven process and going about your day. When you focus on visibility and holistic marketing efforts instead of simply rankings and AEO optimizations, you are future-proofing your efforts and, most importantly, your career.

AI is powerful, no doubt about it. It can automate research, help draft content, or identify patterns in search behavior. But it cannot replace strategy, creativity, or human judgment. AI does not build relationships with your client's customers. It does not create communities. It does not generate word-of-mouth referrals. These are the elements that sustain traffic and brand authority over time.

In short, AI is a complement, not a replacement. Think of it as a tool in your toolkit, not the whole toolbox.

The New Mindset for SEO Professionals

So what does this mean for you as an SEO professional? It means expanding your focus. Yes, continue to optimize websites, structure content, and stay aware of AI trends. But also think beyond search engines. Ask yourself questions like:

- How can my client build authority in their niche that lasts, regardless of algorithm changes?
- Are we helping them develop relationships with their audience that create loyalty and advocacy?
- Are there ways to get visibility and engagement outside traditional search channels?

The businesses that succeed in this new era are not the ones chasing every AI trend. They are the ones investing in real, meaningful connections with their audience. They understand that SEO is one part of a larger marketing strategy.

Last Thoughts

SEO is not dead; it is evolving. Your skills are still relevant. AI can enhance your work, but it cannot replace organic marketing fundamentals. Instead, focus on building visibility, authority, and relationships that last. The role of an SEO professional is becoming more strategic, more holistic, and more valuable.

So, as you finish this chapter, remember this: AI is a powerful tool, but it cannot replace the human-driven aspects of marketing. Your value as an SEO professional is not in chasing every new trend or tactic. It is in helping your clients build lasting visibility, meaningful relationships, and authority that cannot be easily replaced.

Think of AI as a helper, not a replacement. The fundamentals you already know, understanding audiences, creating valuable content, fostering trust, and building long-term relationships, remain as critical as ever.

By embracing this mindset, you are preparing yourself and your clients for success in an AI-driven world, without losing sight of what truly matters.

Chapter 2: Balancing AI Tools with Organic Strategy

Okay, so as you can see, AI is undeniably reshaping the SEO marketing landscape. From content generation to data analysis, AI tools can definitely help you save time and provide insights that were once difficult or impossible to obtain.

But like I said, relying solely on AI for strategy or execution can be dangerous. True success comes from **balancing AI capabilities with organic marketing fundamentals**. For SEO professionals, this balance is crucial. AI can optimize tasks, analyze data, or suggest improvements, but again, it cannot replace judgment, creativity, or relationship-building — that's where you come in.

Why Balance Matters

I was talking about this a bit towards the end of Chapter 1, when I was talking about how agencies were starting to use AI tools to do content. Now, unless you live under a rock, I am sure you can tell that an over-reliance on AI can lead to cookie-cutter content, shallow engagement, and a focus on metrics rather than meaningful results.

But, Organic marketing strategies, on the other hand, prioritize **authority**, **trust**, and **human connection**—elements that AI cannot fully replicate.

By balancing AI and organic approaches, you can ensure that your:

- Content remains valuable and audience-focused
- Marketing efforts are sustainable and adaptable
- SEO and organic growth continue to thrive even if AI trends shift

Essentially, by taking this approach instead of an AI-driven one, you make yourself more flexible and less rigid. By adapting your strategies to fit your clients and their customers, rather than relying on set-it-and-forget-it AI tactics, you make yourself more valuable and better able to deliver results that keep your clients paying.

Practical Ways to Balance AI and Organic Marketing

Now, let's explore some strategies to help SEO professionals integrate AI tools without losing sight of organic priorities:

- **Use AI for Research, Not Creativity**
  AI can analyze keywords, trends, and competitors, but creative direction and messaging should remain human-driven. So, sorry, AI hasn't and won't replace a strong writer.

- **Enhance, Don't Replace**
  Use AI to streamline repetitive tasks such as title tags, meta descriptions, formatting, or data collection—but ensure all output is reviewed, refined, and tailored by humans. So don't throw out your spreadsheets and spell checkers just yet.

- **Maintain Audience Focus**
  AI-generated content or suggestions should always be evaluated through the lens of your client's audience. Does it provide value? Does it answer real questions? Would you actually read the piece of content and feel like you got all your needs met? These are the type of questions you should be asking yourself before you just go putting out a piece of content.

- **Combine AI Insights with Experience**
  Use AI data to inform strategy, but leverage your expertise to make decisions about priorities, opportunities, and messaging. So, being a skilled SEO manager or director still matters.

- **Regularly Audit AI Output**
  AI tools are only as good as the inputs they receive. So if you aren't starting with a strong knowledge base, the AI is just going to give you content that is shallow and regurgitated. So check outputs for accuracy, relevance, and tone to maintain quality

and brand integrity. But, also take the time to consult with actual professionals so you can "train" the AI to deliver insights that are above and beyond the normal slop on the SERPs these days.

Integrating AI into SEO is about efficiency, not substitution. AI can assist with analysis, content ideas, and reporting, allowing SEO professionals to focus on strategy, creativity, and relationship-building. Proper integration strengthens organic efforts rather than replacing them.

Last Thoughts

The key to thriving in an AI-driven SEO marketing landscape is balance. AI tools can amplify your efforts, but they are not a substitute for the human expertise, strategy, and creativity that drive real results.

As an SEO professional, approach AI as a helper, not a replacement. Integrate its capabilities into your organic strategy, but maintain focus on meaningful engagement, authority, and audience connection. By striking the right balance, you ensure that your clients benefit from AI without sacrificing the fundamentals that sustain long-term growth.

Okay, so now that we talked about the New AI SEO landscape and how to navigate that, and how to better strategize, let's now dive a bit deeper into some specific organic marketing strategies.

So we are going to look at organic marketing strategies that align with the three pillars of SEO: Link-Building/Off-Page SEO, On-Page SEO, and Technical SEO. In terms of organic marketing, I am going to refer to Off-Page SEO as "Authority building", On-Page SEO as "Trust building," and Technical SEO as "Reliability" (or Foundation/Infrastructure building).

So a neat way to think about it:

- **Off-Page SEO (Authority)** = What others say about you.
- **On-Page SEO (Trust)** = What you say about yourself.
- **Technical SEO (Reliability/Infrastructure)** = Whether your house is in order so people can actually visit, stay, and return.

So, with that said, let's start with Authority building.

Chapter 3: Building Authority in an AI World

As an SEO professional, you know that rankings can fluctuate. One day, a client is on page one, the next, they're slipping down. Algorithms change, AI evolves, and even paid campaigns cannot guarantee long-term results.

That's why building authority is so critical. So, yes, Off-Page SEO still matters — true authority still lasts. It outperforms temporary trends, drives trust with audiences, and naturally supports search visibility.

Brand authority is more than a logo, tagline, or fancy website. It's also more than some lazy, linked-up, brand mention on a loosely relevant blog post. It's the perception that your client knows their space, delivers value consistently, and can be trusted.

Authority is what keeps customers coming back, generates word-of-mouth referrals, and creates an ecosystem where AI or algorithm changes have less impact.

Why Authority Matters in the AI Era

AI may analyze content and surface answers for users, but it cannot replicate human trust. People still make decisions based on who they know, who they respect, and who they trust. If your client is seen as a credible authority, users will actively seek them out, share their content, and engage with their brand, regardless of algorithmic shifts or whether or not some AI chatbot wants to cite them or not.

For SEO professionals, authority works in your favor. Strong authority drives natural backlinks, social mentions, and signals that search engines interpret as trustworthy. In other words, authority enhances your SEO efforts without having to chase every update or AI trick.

Ways to Build Authority

Here are practical ways to help clients establish lasting authority. To be honest, these are basic public relations tactics, but I'm sharing them to highlight how they remain relevant even in an AI-driven world:

- **Thought Leadership Content**
  Encourage clients to create content that demonstrates expertise, not just targeted keywords. Whitepapers, in-depth guides, case studies, and opinion pieces are all ways to show authority. So, let's avoid the basic questions keywords, listed posts, FAQs, and optimizing for AI overviews, and instead go back to having your clients share real stories and actionable insights.

- **Public Presence**
  Speaking at conferences, webinars, podcasts, or community events positions your client as a leader. Even small appearances or online sessions

contribute to visibility and credibility. So just sitting back and being an “internet-talker” is not enough; encourage your clients to get boots on the ground.

- **Media Mentions**
  Features in industry publications, interviews, and expert quotes still add credibility. Help clients identify opportunities to be featured and provide guidance for outreach.

- **Testimonials and Case Studies**
  Social proof is authority in action. Highlight client successes, share stories, and leverage customer endorsements to build trust. Don’t just ride off on ranking high on search engines; that doesn’t matter as much anymore. People don’t just get stuck on the first couple of results — they explore. So have real data and insights to ensure that when customers do get to your content, they actually stay.

- **Consistency and Reliability**
  Authority is built over time. Consistent content, dependable service, and clear messaging help audiences trust a brand long term. Using AI to spam forums is not going to work; a client’s customers can smell B.S. and tell if the client is just putting up a façade, so taking the time to actually make sure things are cohesive and authentic still matters.

Like I said, authority and SEO go hand in hand. Search engines reward signals of trust: backlinks, mentions, citations, and engagement. But more importantly, authority ensures that even if search rankings fluctuate, the brand maintains recognition and trust.

Your work as an SEO professional becomes less about chasing algorithms and more about amplifying real influence.

Last Thoughts

As you work with clients, always remember that authority is your strongest defense against volatility. Rankings will always change, AI will always evolve, but trust and credibility endure. Authority is not built overnight; it requires consistent effort, thought leadership, and authentic engagement with your audience.

Don’t just tell your clients that building a few links is enough. Share these tactics with them, and have a real conversation about what it takes to build a strong organic presence.

Again, you have to be willing to put boots on the ground. Just sitting back and emailing blog owners for links doesn’t work anymore; you've got to actually work with your client to get their name out there. Off-Page SEO tactics can guide the process, but it can’t do the work for you.

Your role as an SEO professional is to guide clients in building this authority. Show them how to create content that demonstrates expertise, seek opportunities to be recognized publicly, and maintain consistent messaging.

By focusing on authority, you can help clients weather the uncertainties of the AI-driven world and secure sustainable growth, without wasting your time or theirs on meaningless AI-focused optimizations.

Chapter 4: Building Trust in an AI World

Okay, now that we talked about Off-Page SEO/ Authority building, let's now talk about On-Page SEO/ Trust building.

As AI-driven tools become more prevalent in marketing and search, one thing remains clear: **trust is irreplaceable**. No algorithm or automated system can replicate the confidence and credibility a brand earns from genuine relationships with its audience.

For SEO professionals, helping clients build and maintain trust is essential—not just for engagement, but for long-term growth and authority.

Trust in the AI era is earned through transparency, consistency, and reliability. Users and clients want to know that the content they encounter is accurate, valuable, and reflective of human judgment, and not just some rehash of a post that's already out.

Building trust is no longer optional; it is a competitive advantage in a world where AI-generated content can be abundant, but meaningful, reliable guidance is scarce.

Why Building Trust Still Matters

Don't let all the AI crap posts you see on search engines fool you — even though they rank high, they often don't get clicked on. Why? Because audiences don't trust them. Search engines and AI can surface content, but they cannot vouch for credibility beyond signals such as backlinks, engagement, or citations.

Human perception drives loyalty, repeat engagement, and referrals. Trusted brands benefit from:

- Increased conversions and customer retention
- Higher engagement with content and campaigns
- Greater organic sharing and mentions
- Resilience against misinformation or algorithmic changes

For SEO, trust translates into both direct and indirect benefits. When a brand is trusted, audiences engage more deeply, naturally generate backlinks, and provide social signals that search engines recognize. Again, there is no possible way this can be replicated with just a few ChatGPT prompts.

Practical Strategies to Build Trust

With that being said, here are some strategies to help clients maintain credibility and trust in this new AI world we live in:

- **Transparency in Content**
  Clearly cite sources, provide context, and ensure information is accurate. Avoid misleading headlines or over-optimized content that sacrifices clarity. Also, it is okay to use AI to write your content, but you should always take the time to prune it and make sure it actually delivers on its promise.

- **Consistency Across Channels**
  Align messaging, tone, and branding across websites, email campaigns, social platforms, and offline channels. Consistency reinforces credibility. AI can help with this by using it to "modify" the message to each platform, but you still have to make sure that your message actually "appeals" to each specific platform you are targeting, so, in other words, skillful copywriting and salesmanship still matter.

- **Engage Directly with Audiences**
  Respond to questions, address concerns, and participate in meaningful discussions. Personalized engagement builds loyalty. Don't just rely on the post you already see being made; break the mold

and explore topics that aren't being discussed.

- **Showcase Expertise**
  Share case studies, success stories, or detailed insights that demonstrate experience and authority in the field. Again, this is why you need to still be consulting with industry professionals; this ensures that jargon and ideas shared are not only up to date, but also relevant to the people reading the content.

- **Protect User Experience**
  Ensure websites and platforms are secure, easy to navigate, and free of deceptive or intrusive elements. A positive user experience reinforces trust. So again, taking the time to use copywriting methods still matters; AI is just going to dump out text, but it's up to you as the SEO to make it flow and deliver conversions.

As you can see, trust supports SEO indirectly. Backlinks, social mentions, and engagement often result from an audience that believes in the brand. High-quality, trusted content is more likely to be shared, referenced, and linked naturally, all of which strengthen organic visibility.

So again, don't just rely on ChatGPT to rewrite or rehash content already out; go back to tackling content creation through real storytelling and unique insights. AI overviews will catch up.

Last Thoughts

In a world where AI can generate content instantly, trust is what sets a brand apart. Search engines may deliver traffic, and AI may assist with production, but meaningful human connections create loyalty, engagement, and authority that no machine can replicate.

As an SEO professional, your role is to help clients establish and maintain trust across all channels. Emphasize accuracy, consistency, and audience engagement.

By prioritizing trust, you ensure that your client's brand remains relevant, credible, and resilient in the AI era. Now, let's explore the last pillar/component, and that is Technical SEO, but in terms of organic marketing, we are talking about maintaining reliability.

Chapter 5: Building Reliability in an AI World

Now that we've explored Off-Page SEO/Authority building and On-Page SEO/Trust building, it's time to look at Technical SEO through the lens of organic marketing. In practical terms, Technical SEO is about **reliability**—making sure your client's website and digital presence are dependable, accessible, and functional. Without a strong foundation, both trust and authority can falter, no matter how good the content or outreach may be.

Why Reliability Matters

In a world increasingly influenced by AI and evolving search algorithms, the user experience is non-negotiable. A website that is slow, poorly structured, or difficult to navigate undermines trust, frustrates visitors, and limits the impact of all other marketing efforts.

Reliability ensures that audiences can consistently access content, products, and services without friction. If you are an SEO professional reading this, I am sure you know that reliability translates into stability. Technical issues can reduce visibility, limit engagement, and hurt conversions.

By proactively maintaining a dependable infrastructure, you protect the investments made in authority and trust while reinforcing the client's brand.

I also want to mention that, again, while AI is doing most of the work with building websites, the SEO professional is still needed to ensure that the website gives a great experience to users on a consistent basis.

Practical Strategies to Build Reliability

Building reliability requires ongoing effort and structured processes. The following strategies help ensure that your client's website remains stable, secure, and prepared to support all other SEO and marketing efforts:

- **Continue to Conduct Regular Technical Audits**: Monitor site speed, crawl errors, and security issues. Proactively addressing problems prevents small issues from becoming large ones. Now, again, AI can help you fix these things, but it's not going to monitor them; you have to do that.

- **Prioritize Mobile and Accessibility**: With more users accessing content on mobile devices, reliable mobile performance and accessible design are essential. AI can make a damn good mobile website, but again, it's up to you to ensure that it continues to deliver the experience that customers want.

- **Don't Overly Focus On Implementing Structured Data**: Schema Markup doesn't matter, or honestly has never mattered as much as you think. Instead, spend more time making sure your content can be read by searchers, and AI will figure it out. So, in other words, don't waste any more time focusing on structured data; users can't see it anyway, so just focus on other stuff and let the search engines catch up.

- **Monitor and Optimize Hosting and Infrastructure**: Reliable servers and hosting environments prevent downtime and ensure a consistent user experience. Again, AI can build the website, but it's not thinking about your unique hosting or server situation, so you do still need to make sure you choose good hosting, or recommend good hosting to clients.

- **Plan for Growth**: Anticipate traffic spikes, content expansion, and evolving user needs to maintain reliability over time. This is where AI definitely helps save time with making HTML, CSS, and JavaScript templates or code modifications. But again, you still need a skilled web developer and SEO to ensure these changes are appropriate and actually deliver results.

Reliability underpins all other SEO efforts. Authority and trust can drive visitors to a site, but without a technically sound foundation, engagement will suffer, and conversions may decline.

Reliable websites support SEO by ensuring content is discoverable, accessible, and functional, amplifying the impact of content and outreach.

Last Thoughts

In this new AI world, reliability is the pillar that allows trust and authority to shine. Users and clients expect seamless, secure, and accessible experiences. Technical SEO is no longer just a behind-the-scenes task—it is the backbone of sustainable organic marketing.

As an SEO professional, your role is to guide clients in maintaining a dependable digital infrastructure. Ensure that content, products, and services are always accessible, navigation is intuitive, and performance is optimized. Reliability strengthens authority, supports trust, and protects the long-term success of your client's digital presence.

With trust, authority, and reliability aligned, your client is positioned to thrive in an AI-driven landscape without sacrificing the core principles of effective organic marketing.

Chapter 6: Putting It All Together

After exploring strategies ranging from community-led growth and strategic partnerships to human creativity, AI integration, and trust-building, it's time to synthesize these lessons into a holistic approach.

Organic marketing is not just a set of tactics—it is a system. Each component reinforces the others, creating sustainable growth that endures in an AI-driven landscape.

Thinking holistically means integrating every part of the strategy. AI tools, creative content, partnerships, and engagement all work together to drive results for clients and for yourself.

The goal is not just to optimize for search engines or algorithms, but to create value for real audiences while maintaining visibility and authority.

Below, I included a few paragraphs that synthesize and codify each of the organic marketing strategies we discussed in this book into a cohesive "Holistic approach" or strategy that you can follow.

Core Elements of a Holistic Approach

Like I've been saying throughout this book; a fragmented approach—focusing only on rankings, AI optimization, or content production—limits impact.

By understanding the interdependence of each element, you can deliver results that are sustainable, measurable, and meaningful.

Here are the core elements of a Holistic strategy:

1. **Content and Creativity**
   High-quality, valuable content remains the foundation. Creativity ensures it stands out and resonates with audiences. Like I said, AI can help you draft content, but the true creativity comes from a skilled writer.

2. **Community and Engagement**
   Building relationships and fostering discussions strengthens trust, loyalty, and natural amplification. So again, ditch the old, outdated link-building methods, shut down the computer screen, and go back to having real conversations and creating real connections with people.

3. **AI Integration and Maintaining Reliability**
   Use AI tools strategically to enhance efficiency, insights, and data-driven decision-making, without replacing human judgment. Like I said, AI can help fix reliability issues, but a good SEO professional is still needed to sniff out problems and avoid future pitfalls.

4. **Measurement and Adaptation**
   Continue to track meaningful metrics—engagement, conversions, authority signals—and refine strategies based on results rather than just rankings. I didn't spend a lot of time talking about SEO data metrics because they are not that important in an AI age, where authenticity matters even more. So enough of treating users like lab rats and instead focus on seeing them as individuals that each require unique marketing and focus. So again, AI can be used to make connections, but again, you, as the SEO professional, have to be able to know what to do with the data and insights once you get them.

5. **Long-Term Focus**
   Emphasize sustainable growth over short-term gains, preparing clients for changes in algorithms, AI, and user behavior. Help them understand that getting to the top of search engines doesn't matter anymore, and having as many clicks on your website as possible doesn't matter either — help them see that the amount of traffic is not what's important, but the quality and the ability to actually convert it into business opportunities is what really matters now.

Much like superheroes teaming up — when combined, these elements form a system that is greater than the sum of its parts. SEO becomes more than optimizations and a dumping ground for AI tools—and it instead becomes a strategy for lasting authority, engagement, and growth.

Each piece supports the others: creative content fuels communities, communities amplify partnerships, partnerships strengthen authority, and trust and reliability ensure everything resonates with audiences.

Key Takeaways

- Organic marketing is most effective when treated as an integrated system, not isolated tactics.
- Every component—content, creativity, communities, partnerships, AI, measurement, reliability, and trust—works together.
- Holistic approaches increase resilience, authority, and sustainable growth.
- You are the architect of this system, ensuring your clients thrive in an AI-driven world.

Last Thoughts

Holistic organic marketing is the path to long-term success. AI may shape tools and platforms, but human-driven strategy, creativity, and relationship-building remain the foundation.

As an SEO professional, your role is to orchestrate every element of the strategy. Help clients align content, engagement, partnerships, AI integration, and trust-building into a coherent system. By thinking holistically, you create sustainable, measurable, and meaningful growth—ensuring your clients not only survive, but thrive, in the AI era.

Conclusion

As we reach the end of this book, one thing is clear: AI is changing the SEO and marketing landscape as a whole, but it does not replace the fundamentals of organic growth.

SEO professionals still hold a unique and essential role—one that combines strategy, creativity, human connection, and technical insight. Thriving in this new era requires balance, adaptability, and a focus on what truly drives meaningful results.

To remain effective, SEO professionals must focus on future-proofing strategies—building systems, practices, and approaches that endure shifts in technology, user behavior, and search algorithms.

Future-proof SEO is not about predicting every AI development. It's about creating resilient strategies, prioritizing quality and authority, and ensuring that marketing efforts are adaptable to whatever comes next. This approach positions your clients for long-term growth, even as the AI landscape evolves.

With that said, my book has explored the full spectrum of modern organic marketing—from community-led growth and strategic partnerships to creativity, AI integration, trust-building, and long-term strategy. Each chapter emphasized a core principle: AI is a tool, not a substitute. Your expertise, judgment, and human-centric approach are what create lasting success for your clients.

Key Lessons to Remember

Here are some key lessons I want you to take with you as you continue navigating this new SEO landscape. They are basically a summarization of the key points I shared with you in this book.

- **Organic marketing remains essential**
  AI cannot replace the value of real human engagement, relationship-building, and trusted authority.

- **Creativity is irreplaceable**
  While AI can generate content or analyze patterns, only humans can create ideas that resonate emotionally and culturally.

- **Balance AI with strategy**
  Use AI tools to enhance efficiency and insights, but ensure that decisions and direction remain human-driven.

- **Focus on trust and credibility**
  Transparent, consistent, and reliable practices build loyalty, engagement, and authority—elements that

AI cannot manufacture.

- **Measure what matters**
  Go beyond rankings. Track engagement, conversions, and authority signals to understand real impact.

- **Think holistically and long-term**
  Integrate all elements—content, partnerships, creativity, AI, measurement, and trust—into a system designed for sustainable growth.

- **Adapt to AI-driven user behavior**
  Understand how AI shapes discovery and engagement, but prioritize human needs and intent in every strategy.

AI will continue to evolve, creating new tools, platforms, and behaviors. However, the core principles of SEO and organic marketing remain unchanged. Success comes from understanding people, delivering value, and applying expertise with creativity and strategy.

Your role is more important than ever. You are the bridge between technology, human behavior, and business results. By applying the lessons in this book, you can guide clients and yourself through uncertainty, leverage AI effectively, and ensure sustainable growth that withstands changes in algorithms, AI tools, and user behavior.

Last Words

The AI era is not a threat—it is an opportunity for growth. It challenges SEO professionals to think strategically, creatively, and holistically. By focusing on human-centric principles, long-term value, and meaningful engagement, you can help your clients and yourself succeed while strengthening your own expertise and relevance in this evolving landscape.

AI may change the tools, but it cannot replace insight, judgment, or the ability to create meaningful connections. SEO professionals who embrace this mindset will not just survive—they will lead in the AI-driven world of marketing. I hope this book helps you out, and best of luck on your journey! Until next time, take care!

About the Author

Roggie (Raj) Clark is a 10-year SEO professional and owner of the SEO agency, *Bounce Rank.* Prior to joining the SEO industry, Raj was a web developer and school teacher. It was through creating his own websites and wanting a career change from teaching that Raj stumbled across the world of SEO.

Since joining the field nearly a decade ago, Raj has worked on a wide range of campaigns, from e-commerce to B2B to Healthcare, for enterprise companies and marketing agencies in the United States.

He is regarded as an expert and guru by his colleagues and the SEO industry. Raj currently lives in Odenton, Maryland, with his sister and niece.

www.ingramcontent.com/pod-product-compliance
Lightning Source LLC
LaVergne TN
LVHW022323200926
848481LV00004B/1411